D0938627

Cuban AMERICANS

Our CULTURAL HERITAGE

SPIRIT
of America®

Cuban Americans

By Deborah Cannarella

Content Adviser: María R. Estorino, Project Director,
Cuban Heritage Digital Collection

The Child's World®
Chanhassen, Minnesota

8

Cuban AMERICANS

Published in the United States of America by The Child's World®
PO Box 326 • Chanhassen, MN 55317-0326 • 800-599-READ • www.childsworld.com

Acknowledgments
The Child's World®: Mary Berendes, Publishing Director

For Editorial Directions, Inc.: E. Russell Primm, Editorial Director; Sarah E. De Capua and Pam Rosenberg, Line Editors; Elizabeth K. Martin, Assistant Editor; Olivia Nellums, Editorial Assistant; Susan Hindman, Copy Editor; Joanne Mattern, Proofreader; Matthew Messbarger, Ann Grau Duvall, and Deborah Grahame, Fact Checkers; Tim Griffin/IndexServ, Indexer; Cian Loughlin O'Day, Photo Researcher; Linda S. Koutris, Photo Selector

Photos
Cover/frontispiece: Hulton-Deutsch Collection/Corbis

Cover photographs ©: Corbis

Interior photographs ©: Bettmann/Corbis: 6, 8, 11, 14, 16, 25; Corbis: 7 (Kevin Fleming), 13, 15 (John Olson), 17 (Nik Wheeler), 18 (Nathan Benn), 20 (Reuters NewMedia Inc.), 22 (Timothy Fadek); Getty Images: 19 (Tim Chapman/Miami Herald), 28 (Robert Nickelsber/Liason); Getty Images/Hulton Archive: 12, 26-bottom; Nik Wheeler/Corbis: 17, 24; Reuters NewMedia Inc./Corbis: 20, 26-top, 27; Stocker Susan/Corbis Sygma: 23-bottom; Tony Arruza/Corbis: 10, 23-top.

Registration
The Child's World®, Spirit of America®, and their associated logos are the sole property and registered trademarks of The Child's World®.

Library of Congress Cataloging-in-Publication Data
Cannarella, Deborah.
  Cuban Americans / by Deborah Cannarella.
    p. cm. — (Our cultural heritage)
"Spirit of America."
Contents: The first Cubans in America—Making a new home—A changing community—Cuban Americans today.
  ISBN 1-59296-013-8 (lib. bdg. : alk. paper)
  1. Cuban Americans—Juvenile literature. [1. Cuban Americans.] I. Title. II. Series.
E184.C97C36 2003
973'.04687291—dc21
                                   2003004286

Contents

Chapter ONE

The First Cubans in America

PEOPLE HAVE BEEN COMING TO SETTLE IN America for thousands of years. Even today, many people still travel from other countries to make the United States their home. These **immigrants** come for many reasons. Some come to find freedom. Others come to find new and better ways to live. The people of Cuba came to America for both of these reasons.

The U.S. Coast Guard helping Cuban refugees get off a boat in Key West, Florida, in 1965

Cuba is the largest island in the West Indies. It is only 90 miles (145 kilometers)

from Key West, one of the islands of Florida. The waterway that separates Cuba from the United States is called the Straits of Florida.

Because their countries are close neighbors, the people of Cuba and the United States have always had strong ties. At one time, Spain owned both Cuba and Florida. After Spain sold Florida to the United States, many Cubans came to the United States to escape the Spanish rulers.

Later, many Cubans came to the United States to work. Cuban cigar makers built factories in New York and Florida. In 1886, Vincente Martínez Ybor opened a cigar factory near Tampa, Florida. Soon, many other Cubans opened factories there, too. The area became known as Ybor City, or "Cigar City."

By 1900, more than 11,000 Cubans lived and worked in factories in the United States. The factory owners ran ferryboats from Florida to Cuba. The workers could travel back and forth whenever they wished.

A worker making cigars in a factory in Ybor City near Tampa, Florida

7

Cuba became an independent country in 1902. Cubans continued to visit the United States as tourists and students. Many Americans traveled to Cuba on vacation, too. Airplanes made regular flights from Havana—the capital of Cuba—to Miami, Florida.

In 1959, Fidel Castro took over the government of Cuba. Thousands of people who did not support Castro suddenly had to leave their country. In three years, more than 200,000 Cubans came to the United States.

Many of these immigrants were wealthy and had good jobs in Cuba. They were teachers, doctors, lawyers, bankers, and other professional people. As they left their country, Castro took their houses, cars, and property. Because these people were once rich and successful, they were called the Golden **Exiles.**

Castro did not allow everyone to leave Cuba. An American priest named Bryan Walsh wanted to help the children whose

Fidel Castro speaking to the crowds as he took control of Cuba's government in 1959

parents could not leave. Even though it was difficult to send a child to the United States alone, many parents wanted their children to grow up in a free country. Freedom was not possible in Cuba where everyone was expected to agree with Castro's ideas or suffer the consequences.

In 1960, Walsh and the U.S. government started a program in Miami called Operation Pedro Pan. The program was named after the imaginary character Peter Pan. *Pedro* is Spanish for "Peter." Pedro was also the name of the first child that Walsh helped in Miami. Walsh worked with James Baker, the headmaster of a school in Havana. Baker got the children out of Cuba, and Walsh helped them when they arrived in Florida.

In one year, Operation Pedro Pan flew more than 14,000 children into Miami. Many of the children traveled alone. Some were only three or four years old. Most of the children lived in foster families around the United States until their parents could leave Cuba and join them.

Most of the Cubans who arrived in the United States stayed in Florida. The warm

Cuban dance is a mix of Spanish, African, and Caribbean styles. Some traditional dances are the *danzón* and the rumba. Popular dances include the cha-cha, mambo, and salsa.

Calle Ocho is a well-known street in the Cuban community known as Little Havana in Miami, Florida.

weather, tall palm trees, and buildings reminded them of Cuba. They also wanted to remain close to their country. They thought Castro would soon lose power. Then they would be able to return to the island.

The Cubans lived together in a small section of downtown Miami. The neighborhood later became known as Little Havana. They were glad to have their friends and relatives nearby. Together, they could share their favorite Cuban meals, speak in their native Spanish language, and tell stories of their lives back home. They helped each other adjust to life in the new land. The Cuban Americans are still a strong community today.

The exiles arrived in the United States with very little money or personal property. However, they brought with them their many skills and talents, the spirit to work hard—and the dream of one day returning home.

10

FIDEL CASTRO RUZ WAS BORN ON AUGUST 13, 1926. His father was a successful sugar farmer from Spain. When Castro was a young man, he worked in his family's sugarcane fields.

Castro studied law at the University of Havana. He wanted to work in Cuba's government. Before he could run for election, however, Fulgencio Batista took over the government.

Castro did not agree with Batista's ideas. He tried to force Batista out of power. As a result, Castro was captured and then sent to prison. He became a hero to farmers, workers, and students. After he was released from prison, Castro led rebels against Batista in the Cuban Revolution. When Batista finally left Cuba, Castro succeeded in taking over the government. In 1960, Castro **allied** Cuba with the Soviet Union.

He turned Cuba into the first **communist** nation in the Western Hemisphere. Soon, people saw that Castro was not the leader they hoped he would be. He built schools, hospitals, and apartments. He also took away people's land and businesses. He took control of the newspapers and the radio and television stations. He did not allow anyone to speak out against him. Today, Cubans are not allowed to leave the island without special permission. Americans are also not allowed to visit without special permission.

Castro has been Cuba's leader since 1959. He is the only political leader in the world who has been in power for such a long time. Many Cuban Americans are still waiting for him to leave so that they may visit their homeland.

11

Chapter Two

Making a New Home

Prisoners captured by Castro's troops during the Bay of Pigs invasion

THE GOLDEN EXILES HOPED TO STAY IN Florida for only a short time. They believed that the United States would force Castro out of Cuba. Then they would be able to return home. Castro had become a friend to the Soviet Union, which was an enemy of the United States.

In 1961, the United States trained a group of Cuban exiles for a secret mission. They were going to invade Cuba. However, Castro found out about the plan. In April, the soldiers landed in the Bay of Pigs, an area in south Cuba. In two days, Castro's troops

killed more than 100 soldiers and captured more than 1,000 others.

The next year, U.S. spy planes found missile sites in Cuba. The Soviet Union was sending powerful weapons there. President John F. Kennedy told the Soviet Union to remove the sites, or there would be war. The Soviet leader agreed—but only if the United States promised never to invade Cuba again. This event is called the Cuban Missile Crisis.

After the Cuban Missile Crisis, Cubans could no longer fly from Havana to Miami. Many relatives of the first exiles—and of the

President John F. Kennedy (front and center) held meetings with U.S. Army officials during the Cuban Missile Crisis in 1962.

Refugees being given forms to fill out at the Cuban Refugee Emergency Center in Miami, Florida, in 1965

children of Pedro Pan—were still on the island. In September 1965, Castro let more Cubans leave by boat. Exiles in Florida sailed to Camarioca, Cuba, to pick up their relatives. About 5,000 Cubans landed in Florida in just two months. Many others drowned or were stranded at sea.

President Lyndon Johnson wanted to find a safer way for people to leave the island. Castro agreed that two flights could leave Cuba each day. These flights were called the Freedom Flights. The Freedom Flights continued for eight years. Almost 300,000 Cubans arrived in Miami between 1965 and 1973.

The Cubans in America began to lose hope. They no longer believed the United States would be able to remove Castro from power. They knew they would not return home for a long time. So, they decided to build new lives in the United States.

Many of the Cubans opened markets, restaurants, flower shops, and other businesses in downtown Miami. As more Cubans moved there, the neighborhood grew. Soon, everything the Cubans needed could be found within just a few city blocks. There, the Cubans could live just as they had back home. Eighth Street became known by its Spanish name, Calle Ocho. Little Havana almost seemed like Havana, Cuba, itself.

This bakery is one of many Cuban-owned businesses in the Little Havana neighborhood of Miami.

Living and working together made the Cuban community strong. The Cubans worked hard to succeed. Soon, Miami grew from a small town to a thriving city. By the 1970s, Cubans owned more than 33 of every 100 businesses in Miami. By the 1980s, Miami was an international business center. The Cubans had both the language and the skills to work with large companies in Spanish-speaking countries.

15

Tony Perez, a Cuban-American baseball player who played for the Cincinnati Reds, taking the oath to become a citizen of the United States

Interesting Fact

▶ Union City, New Jersey, is known as Havana on the Hudson. This city on the Hudson River has the largest Cuban population outside of South Florida.

Many of the Cubans on the Freedom Flights did not stay in South Florida. They settled in other towns throughout the United States. These included New York City, Chicago, Los Angeles, New Orleans, Boston, Washington, D.C., and Union City, New Jersey. Soon, there were Cubans in nearly every state of the country.

Today, there are more than 1 million Cuban Americans in the United States. No matter where they live, many consider Miami the true Cuban center of the country. There, they can find the climate, language, foods, and **culture** that remind them of home.

16

Little Havana is lined with palm trees. The buildings are painted in bright colors and with colorful **murals.** The streets and the **bodegas** are full of music, people, and activity.

Along busy Calle Ocho, vendors sell ice cream, roasted peanuts, fruits, and vegetables. In the tobacco shops, the cigars are hand-rolled, just as they were for hundreds of years in Cuba. The restaurants serve *congrí* (rice and beans), *cubanos* (sandwiches), and *café con leche* (Cuban coffee with milk).

In Domino Park, men in *guayaberas* (lightweight linen or cotton shirts) sit at small tables. They play dominoes, a Chinese game the Spanish brought to Cuba hundreds of years ago. Next to the park is the famous Tower Theatre— one of the first theaters in Miami to show movies with Spanish **subtitles.**

On the last Friday of each month, Little Havana holds a large street festival. On Cultural Friday (*Viernes Cultural*), Calle Ocho is filled with music and dancing. Artists set up their easels. Dancers, poets, and musicians perform in the streets. Thousands of people gather to celebrate the sights, sounds, and spirit of Cuban America.

Chapter THREE

A Changing Community

Second-generation Cuban-American girls at their school in Miami's Little Havana neighborhood

THE FIRST CUBANS TO ARRIVE IN THE United States did not think of themselves as Americans. They thought of themselves as Cubans. They kept their language and traditions alive. They lived, worked, and made friends with other Cubans. They continued to dream of returning "home" someday.

Their children did not all have the same ties to Cuba. Many of them were born in Cuba, but they grew up in the United States. They spoke Spanish in their homes, but they spoke English at school. They learned about Cuba's history and traditions. They were learning about America, too. Some people call these children the "one-and-a-half generation," because they lived between two cultures.

In 1979, Castro allowed the exiles to return to Cuba for a visit—for the first time in

A group of Marielitos arriving in Key West, Florida, in 1980

20 years. About 100,000 Cuban Americans traveled to the island. They brought food, medicine, blue jeans, and televisions to their friends and relatives.

Under Castro's control, Cuba had become very poor. A large number of people did not have enough to eat. When the Cubans heard about life in America, they wanted to leave Cuba, too. In 1980, after a large protest in Havana, Castro once again allowed the Cuban people to leave. The Straits of Florida was filled with boats. One day, more than 6,000 people landed in Florida. About 125,000 Cubans arrived in five months.

Ileana Ros-Lehtinen (right) was the first Hispanic woman elected to the U.S. Congress.

These immigrants sailed from the port of Mariel, so they are called the Marielitos. A large number settled in the city of Hialeah, Florida. Many of them were artists, writers, and musicians. Some of the most famous Marielitos are the poet Reinaldo Arenas, the painter and writer Juan Abreu, and the dancer Juanita Baro. These new arrivals shared their talents in the hundreds of Cuban theaters, galleries, and arts festivals that had opened in Florida.

The Cuban community grew larger and stronger. By 1987, there were so many Cubans in Florida, the *Miami Herald* printed a Spanish edition of the newspaper. The children of the "one-and-a-half generation" became bank presidents, doctors, and lawyers. Many moved out of the small Cuban communities and into American neighborhoods.

Cubans also became leaders in government. In 1989, Ileana Ros-Lehtinen, who was born in Havana, became the first Hispanic woman elected to the U.S. Congress. Robert

Menendez—the first Cuban mayor of Union City, New Jersey—was also elected to Congress. Today, he is the highest-ranking Hispanic in the history of the U.S. Congress.

Conditions for the Cubans in America were improving. Conditions in Cuba, however, were getting worse. For many years, the Soviet Union gave Cuba supplies and money. When the Soviet Union crumbled in 1991, Cuba began to suffer, too. There was not enough food, water, or electricity. Castro allowed more people to leave.

In 1994, thousands risked their lives trying to reach Florida. They sailed on small home-made rafts, Styrofoam pieces, and inner tubes. These immigrants were called *balseros,* or rafters. Many of them died at sea. The *balseros* who arrived safely joined the Cuban community in South Florida. With the help of other Cubans, they found jobs and homes there.

President Bill Clinton decided that Cubans could no longer enter the United States without **visas.** Even with this new law, many people still tried to escape. Those who made it to shore could stay. Those caught in the water were sent back to Cuba.

Interesting Fact

In 1991, José Basulto and other Cuban exiles formed Brothers to the Rescue, a group that saved thousands of people who were nearly lost at sea while trying to escape Cuba on rafts and in homemade boats.

21

In 1999, Florida fishermen found five-year-old Elián González floating in the ocean in an inner tube. The boat that was carrying Elián, his mother, and 12 other people had sunk. Elián's father was in Cuba. He wanted Elián to return there. Elián's relatives in Miami wanted him to stay. In 2000, the U.S. government returned Elián to his father. Thousands of Cuban Americans protested. Like Elián's mother, they had risked their lives to escape Cuba. They did not want to go back, and they did not want Elián to go back, either.

Thousands of Cuban-Americans protested when the U.S. government returned Elián González to his father in Cuba.

These people who left Cuba have made new lives in America. Each group of immigrants, however, still dreams of a free Cuba. Pope John Paul II visited Cuba in 1998. Former president Jimmy Carter visited in 2002. Since those visits, there have been many changes inside and outside of Cuba. Someday, Cuban Americans may be able to return to the beautiful country they remember and love.

FOR MANY CUBANS, FOODS FROM THEIR HOME-
land bring back memories of childhood. For
others, traditional foods are a delicious way to
celebrate Cuba's history and culture.

Cuban cooking is a mix of cooking styles—
native Indian, Spanish, African, and Chinese. All
of these people have lived in Cuba and shaped
its culture. The native people of Cuba grew
corn—a key ingredient in *tamales*. *Tamales* are small packets of spicy pork and
cornmeal cooked in corn husks. The Spanish settlers brought *paella*—a spicy
stew of meat, fish, and rice.

The Africans brought the thick root vegetables called *malanga* and *ñame*.
They also cooked with plantain and pumpkin. Today, *maduros* (fried sweet
plantains) are a popular treat. *Arroz frito* (Cuban fried rice) is one example of
the Chinese influence on Cuban cooking. This dish is very much like the fried
rice served in many Chinese restaurants.

A Cuban meal often ends with a delicious dessert—*arroz con leche* (rice
pudding), *buñuelos* (fried
dough with syrup), or
pastelitos de guayaba (pastries
filled with guava). To wash it
all down, Cubans sometimes
drink *guarapos* (fresh sugarcane juice with crushed ice)
and *coco frío* (cold coconut
milk, served straight out of
the shell and sipped through
a straw).

Chapter Four

Cuban Americans Today

Dancers in colorful costumes performing at the Calle Ocho Festival in Little Havana

MORE THAN 1 MILLION CUBANS HAVE ENTERED the United States since 1959. They came at different times and for different reasons. Together, they formed a new community—the Cuban Americans. These people are proud to be Cubans. They are proud to be Americans, too.

Every May 20, Cuban Americans celebrate Cuba's Independence Day. This day marks the day in 1898 when the Cubans won their independence from Spain. They also celebrate many other traditional holidays. When young girls celebrate their 15th birthdays, many have a large party called *La Fiesta de Los Quinces.* Every January, children join the José Martí

24

Parade in Hialeah. José Martí was a famous Cuban poet and hero.

Cuban Americans have started new traditions, too. Each year in March, the Calle Ocho Festival is held in Little Havana. It is the largest Hispanic street festival in the United States. More than 1 million people come to Miami to share the Cuban food, music, and dancing. One year, dancers formed a conga line almost 3 miles (5 km) long!

Many Cuban-American singers and musicians perform at the Calle Ocho Festival. A few of the most famous are Olga Guillot, Willy Chirino, and Gloria Estefan.

Olga Guillot is called the Queen of Bolero. Bolero is a type of traditional Cuban music. Guillot, a singer, left Cuba in 1961. She was one of the first musicians to leave Cuba after Castro took over the country. Three years later, she became the first Hispanic artist to perform at New York City's famous Carnegie Hall.

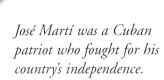

José Martí was a Cuban patriot who fought for his country's independence.

Interesting Fact

Sergio Lopez Mesa is a sculptor whose work celebrates his Cuban background. He was born in Havana and studied art in both Cuba and Italy. He left Cuba during the revolution and moved first to Mexico, then Miami, and finally to Los Angeles. Among his statues are those of José Martí and explorer Christopher Columbus.

Cuban-American singer Gloria Estefan performing in Hollywood, California, in 2002

Willy Chirino came to the United States as a child with Operation Pedro Pan. Today, he is a popular singer and songwriter. He performs a type of **salsa** music known as the Miami Sound—a mix of Cuban music and American rock and jazz.

Gloria Estefan's family left Cuba when she was two years old. She met her husband, Emilio Estefan, when they were in high school. Gloria sang in Emilio's band. They performed at weddings and *Los Quinces* birthday parties. Later, their band, The

Cuban-born performer Desi Arnaz and his wife, Lucille Ball, starred in the television series I Love Lucy.

Miami Sound Machine, became an international success. The couple still lives in Miami. They also own a music and dance club there, called Bongos Cuban Café.

One of the first Cuban performers to become popular in the United States was Desi Arnaz. His family left Cuba in 1933, after President Gerardo Machado was forced to flee. Arnaz's father had supported Machado. Arnaz became a well-known singer and bongo drum player in Miami Beach. Later, he and his wife, Lucille Ball, starred in the popular television series *I Love Lucy* for six years.

One of today's most popular Cuban-American actors is Andy Garcia. He left Havana when he was five years old. After college, he was in a popular television program called *Que Pasa, U.S.A.?* The show was a comedy, in Spanish and English, about a Cuban family living in America. Garcia also starred in *The Godfather: Part III.* He was nominated for an Academy Award. Later, he

Cuban-Americans Andy Garcia and Arturo Sandoval backstage at the sixth annual American Latino Media Arts Awards

produced and starred in a film about Arturo Sandoval, a musician who left Cuba in 1990.

Cuban Americans have also had great success in sports. Many Cuban baseball players have left Cuba to join American teams. Liván Hernández escaped from Cuba in 1995. He pitched for the Florida Marlins when they won the World Series in 1997.

That same year, Hernández's older brother, Orlando, left Cuba in a small boat. Three months later, he became a pitcher for the New York Yankees. The team won three World Series in a row. Orlando got his nickname, El Duque, from his father, who was a famous baseball player in Cuba.

The first Cuban exiles brought the spirit of "old Cuba" to the United States. Their children and grandchildren kept that spirit alive—but they added their own talents and dreams. Theirs is the new spirit of Cuban America.

Cuban Americans exercising their freedom of speech—one of the many freedoms they enjoy in the United States

28

1819 Spain sells Florida to the United States.

1853 Cuban poet and hero José Julián Martí y Perez is born in Havana.

1898 The United States helps Cuba win independence from Spain. After the war, Cuba is under the protection of the United States.

1902 Cuba becomes an independent republic.

1926 Fidel Castro Ruz is born on August 13 near Birán, Cuba.

1952 Fulgencio Batista, a former president of Cuba, takes control of Cuba's government.

1959 Castro takes control of the Cuban government on January 1.

1960 Operation Pedro Pan begins. The first Cuban children arrive in Miami in December.

1961 On April 17, Brigade 2506 lands at the Bay of Pigs in Cuba.

1962 The Cuban Missile Crisis almost leads to war between the United States and the Soviet Union. The crisis lasts 13 days. Cubans are no longer allowed to leave Cuba.

1965 In September, Castro allows Cubans to leave from Camarioca by boat. By November, about 5,000 Cubans arrive in Florida. In December, Cubans start to leave by airplane on the first Freedom Flights.

1973 The last Freedom Flight leaves Havana on April 6. The Tower Theatre in Miami begins to show movies with Spanish subtitles.

1980 Castro allows about 125,000 people to leave Cuba from the port of Mariel.

1985 Miami elects Cuban-born Xavier Suarez as its first Cuban-American mayor.

1987 *The Miami Herald* starts a Spanish-language edition of its newspaper, called *El Nuevo Herald (The New Herald).*

1989 Cuban-born Ileana Ros-Lehtinen becomes the first Hispanic woman in the U.S. Congress.

1994 Tens of thousands of balseros leave Cuba by sea. President Bill Clinton sends them to the U.S. Naval Base at Guantánamo Bay before allowing them into the United States.

1998 Pope John Paul II visits Cuba in January.

1999 A game between the Baltimore Orioles and the Cuban All Stars on March 28 is the first Major League Baseball game played in Cuba since 1959. Elián González is rescued by Florida fishermen on November 25. He is returned to Cuba on April 20, 2000.

2002 Robert Menendez becomes the highest-ranking Hispanic in the history of the U.S. Congress.

allied (AL-ide)
When people or groups are allied, they are joined together for a common purpose. Castro allied Cuba with the Soviet Union.

bodegas (bo-DAY-guhs)
Bodegas are grocery stores that sell foods popular with many Hispanic people. There are many bodegas in Little Havana.

communist (KOM-yuh-nist)
A communist country is one that follows a system of government in which all of the land, factories, houses, and other wealth are controlled by the government. The government is then supposed to make sure that the wealth is shared equally by all citizens. Cuba became the first communist country in the Western Hemisphere.

culture (KUHL-chur)
A culture is a way of life shared by a group of people. Cuban Americans in Little Havana share a common culture.

exiles (EG-siles)
Exiles are people who are forced to leave their home country. The first Cubans to come to the United States after Castro took over their country are sometimes called the Golden Exiles.

immigrants (IM-uh-gruhnts)
Immigrants are people who leave their home countries to live permanently in another country. Immigrants come to the United States for many reasons.

murals (MYU-ruhls)
Murals are large paintings on walls or ceilings. Colorful murals are painted on many buildings in Little Havana.

salsa (SAHL-suh)
Salsa is a type of popular music that combines traditional Spanish musical styles with African rhythms and rock music. Willy Chirino performs a type of salsa music known as the Miami Sound.

subtitles (SUHB-tye-tuhls)
Subtitles are words printed at the bottom of a movie screen. They are the same words spoken by the actors, but translated into a different language. The Tower Theatre was one of the first movie theaters in Miami to show movies with Spanish subtitles.

visas (VEE-zuhz)
Visas are special documents that give a person permission to enter a foreign country. President Clinton decided that Cubans could no longer enter the United States without visas.

Web Sites

Visit our homepage for lots of links about Cuban Americans:
http://www.childsworld.com/links.html

Note to Parents, Teachers, and Librarians:
We routinely verify our Web links to make sure they're safe,
active sites—so encourage your readers to check them out!

Books

Hahn, Laura. *The Cuban Americans.* Philadelphia: Mason Crest Publishers, 2003.

Marvis, Barbara. *Rafael Palmeiro.* Childs, Md.: Mitchell Lane Publishers, Inc., 1998.

Peterson, Tiffany. *Cuban Americans.* Chicago: Heinemann Library, 2003.

Veciana-Suarez, Ana. *Flight to Freedom.* New York: Orchard Books, 2002.

Places to Visit or Contact

Cuban Cultural Center of New York
Times Square Station
P.O. Box 2608
New York, NY 10036

Latin American Art Museum
2206 S.W. Eighth Street
Miami, FL 33135
305/644-1127

Index

About the Author

Deborah Cannarella is an author and editor of history and biography books for children. She is the author of a number of other books for The Child's World® including *Zora Neale Hurston, Langston Hughes,* and *James Baldwin* in the Journey to Freedom® series. Cannarella is also the author and editor of several magazine articles and books for adults. She lives in Roxbury, Connecticut.